MY TIGER LIFE

by Shoshana Stopek
illustrated by Jesga Machado

PICTURE WINDOW BOOKS
a capstone imprint

Published by Picture Window Books,
an imprint of Capstone
1710 Roe Crest Drive
North Mankato, Minnesota 56003
capstonepub.com

Library of Congress Cataloging-in-Publication Data is available on the Library of Congress website.
ISBN: 9798875239496 (hardcover)
ISBN: 9798875239441 (paperback)
ISBN: 9798875239458 (ebook PDF)

Summary: Join a strong and stealthy Bengal tiger as she protects her territory and keeps her cubs healthy and safe.

Editorial Credits
Editor: Christianne Jones
Designer: Kay Fraser
Production Specialist: Whitney Schaefer

Printed and bound in China. PO 6461

Hello! I'm a strong and stealthy Bengal tiger. I live in the dense, green forest of India. I rule as queen of my **territory**. Let's prowl together!

It's dawn, one of the most active times of the day for me.

I sniff around to make sure no other tigers are nearby.

Then I roam my territory, marking trees.

Do I use my scent, claws, or roar to mark my territory?

If you guessed any one of those,
you were right!

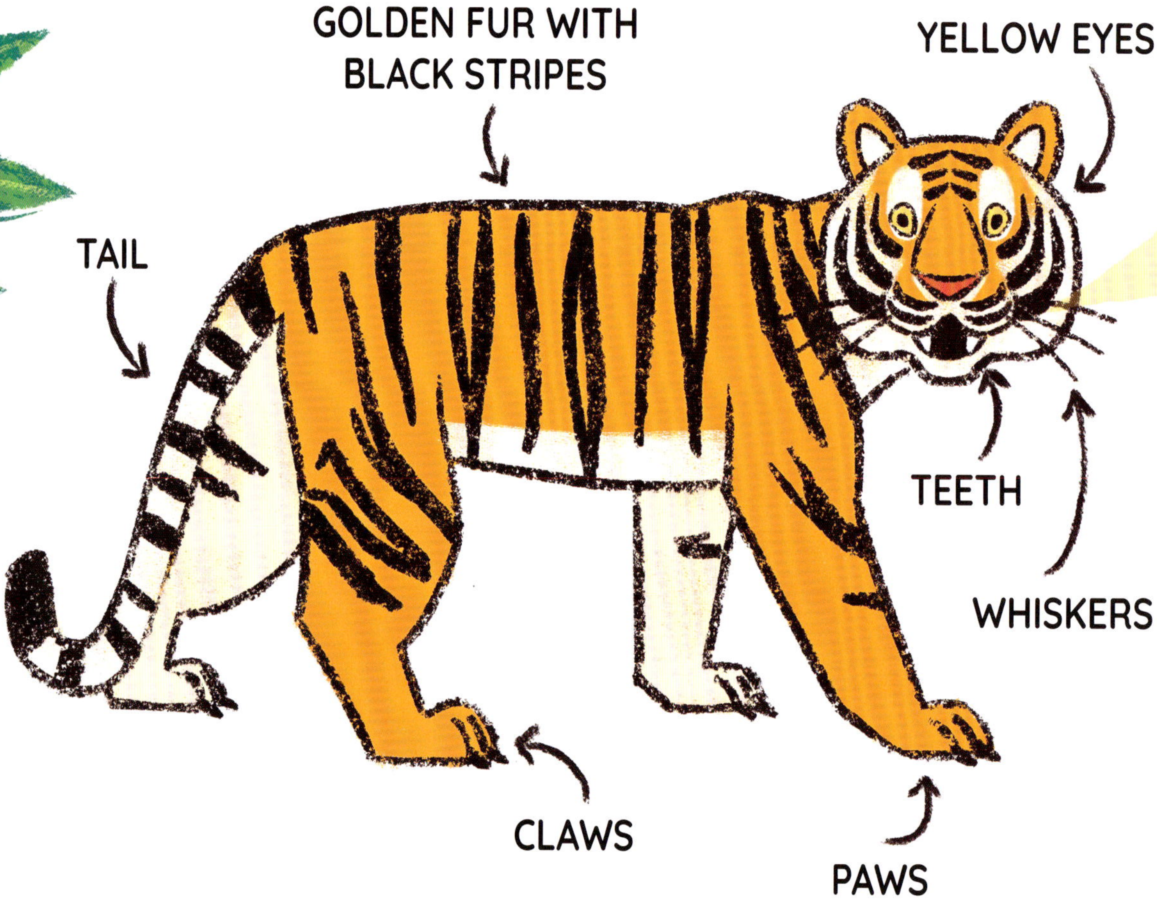

I'm a powerful animal with strong muscles and sharp claws and teeth.

UNIQUE STRIPE PATTERNS

I'm also a beautiful animal with a smooth, striped coat. Each tiger has its own unique stripe pattern.

I don't roar very often. But when I do, my roar can be heard up to two miles away.

I might roar to mark my territory. I also might roar to communicate with another tiger or to attract a mate.

Look at this beautiful forest I live in. Sometimes people cut down trees and build things here. This makes it harder for tigers to find places to live, hunt, and raise their cubs.

Some people also try to hunt tigers and sell their fur. This is called poaching. You can teach everyone how special tigers are and protect us so these things don't happen.

This is my den. It's a cozy, hidden spot where I can rest and keep safe.

I share my den with my cubs. As a female tiger, it's my job to take care of the cubs.

Guess who does all the hunting?

Me! Female tigers are the main hunters and providers for their cubs.

While my cubs are young, I teach them how to hunt, hide, and survive.

How many years do you think my cubs stay with me?

Around two years is the answer. We don't have many enemies, but I keep my cubs close. I protect them from predators like bears and crocodiles.

If a predator spots my den, I have to move my family to a new home.

After a morning of play, it's time to rest. You might not like naps, but I love them! Tigers sleep 18 to 20 hours a day.

Tigers are nocturnal, so when do you think I hunt?

At night! Tigers have an excellent sense of hearing, which helps with night hunting.

But do you know what helps even more?

Our incredible night vision! We can see six times better than humans can see in the dark.

My cubs stay in the den when I hunt.

Tigers are carnivores, which means we only eat meat. Any guesses what I like to hunt?

Deer and wild boar are my favorites. I use my stealth skills to sneak up on prey. My stripes help me blend into my environment, making it easier to hide.

I stay low to the ground while I quietly creep through the grass. I hear movement ahead and spot a boar.

When I'm close enough . . .

. . . I pounce with all my strength!

I return to my den with dinner for my cubs.
They are more than ready to eat!

Now it’s time for some more sleep,
with the soothing sounds of nature
all around us.

Thanks for spending the day—and
night—with me!

Terrific Tiger Facts

- Bengal tigers are also called Indian tigers and Royal Bengal tigers.
- Tigers are members of the cat family. But unlike most cats, tigers like to swim! Their webbed paws help them paddle.
- In one night, tigers may roam up to 20 miles looking for prey. They only need about one meal per week, but they still hunt every day.
- A group of tigers is called a streak or an ambush. A female tiger is called a tigress. A male tiger is just called a tiger.
- Tiger cubs are born blind and only a few survive.
- The white spots on the back of a tiger's ears are called flashes. They look like fake eyes, which confuses other animals. They help cubs follow their mother as well.

Glossary

carnivore (KAHR-nuh-vohr)—an animal that only eats meat

dense (DENS)—thick

environment (en-VAHY-ruhn-muhnt)—the air, water, trees, and other natural surroundings

mark (MAHRK)—to claim territory or communicate by leaving signals like scents or scratches

nocturnal (nok-TUR-nuhl)—active at night

poach (POCH)—to illegally hunt and capture animals

predator (PRED-uh-tor)—an animal that hunts other animals for food

prey (PRAY)—an animal hunted or killed by another animal for food

stealthy (STEL-thee)—secretly

About the Author

Shoshana Stopek is the author of numerous books for all ages, including *Cows Wear Polka Dots* and *Hammock for Two*. She writes books that inspire curiosity, compassion, and connection. When she's not writing, Shoshana works in the entertainment industry and enjoys life in Los Angeles with her family. Visit her at shoshanastopek.com.

About the Illustrator

Jesga Machado graduated with a degree in computer science, but quit her programming career in 2015 to pursue her dream of becoming an illustrator. Since then, she has created artwork for textbooks, picture books, magazines, and board games for clients worldwide. Jesga also created the "Ano do Amigo" project, which produced and sold table calendars for six years to raise funds for an animal shelter in Brazil. Jesga lives in Sorocaba, a city in São Paulo, Brazil.